NO DOUBT THE NAMELESS

Also by Sydney Lea

Poetry

I Was Thinking of Beauty
Six Sundays Toward a Seventh
Young of the Year
Ghost Pain
Pursuit of a Wound
To the Bone: New and Selected Poems
The Blainville Testament
Prayer for the Little City
No Sign
The Floating Candles
Searching the Drowned Man

Fiction

A Place in Mind

Essays

What's the Story? Reflections on a Life Grown Long
A North Country Life: Tales of Woodsmen, Waters, and Wildlife
A Hundred Himalayas
Hunting the Whole Way Home
A Little Wildness

NO DOUBT THE NAMELESS

Sydney Lea

Four Way Books
Tribeca

Copyright © 2016 by Sydney Lea
No part of this book may be used or reproduced in any manner
without written permission except in the case of brief quotations
embodied in critical articles and reviews.

Please direct all inquiries to:
Editorial Office
Four Way Books
POB 535, Village Station
New York, NY 10014
www.fourwaybooks.com

Library of Congress Cataloging-in-Publication Data

Lea, Sydney, 1942-
 [Poems. Selections]
 No doubt the nameless : poems / by Sydney Lea.
    pages ; cm
 ISBN 978-1-935536-73-4 (pbk. : alk. paper)
 I. Title.
 PS3562.E16A6 2016
 811'.54--dc23
                              2015028578

This book is manufactured in the United States of America and printed on acid-free paper.

Four Way Books is a not-for-profit literary press. We are grateful for the assistance
we receive from individual donors, public arts agencies, and private foundations.

This publication is made possible with public funds from the New York State Council on the Arts,
a state agency.

[clmp]

We are a proud member of the Community of Literary Magazines and Presses.

Distributed by University Press of New England
One Court Street, Lebanon, NH 03766

In loving memory of my brother-in-law Amico "Chip" Barone

You were my hero, still are. There seem fewer and fewer
Like you in whose person ethic and deed are combined.
Thought, no matter how lofty, seems duller than lead,
Without heart to match, just as faith without works is dead.
You said, no matter how terribly you were tried,
You felt a lucky man. I remember you'd say
As well—though we all must meet with pain and dread—
The world's best things are happening every day.

In loving memory of my brother-in-law Amico "Chip" Bacone

CONTENTS

I. No Doubt the Nameless

Call Him Zero   3
Anglo-Saxon Dirge   5
The Nightmares You Knew   7
Not In the Photo (1952)   9
Easy to Love   10
Pallid   14
A Man Tells a Story   16
Cooking by Waters: A Non-Elegy   18
How to Sort Them   21

II. Crepuscule

Old Husband's Tale   25
Last Graduate   27
Gate, Beggar, and Birds   29
Heterodox   31
Kansas   32
Woodpile to Shed   34
Crepuscule   36
The Pastor   38
Milton's Satan   39
Winter Poet   41
They'll Leave First   43
Final Evening at Oxbrook Camp   45

III. When the Light Fails

Pariah 49
Old Creatures 51
Locals 53
When the Light Fails 66
She Recalls a Book of Sayings 68
Outsider 70
Solitary 73
Home 74
Forever 77
Blues for the Tenor Man 80
Autumn 83
Who Knows? That Lifelong Question 85

IV. Victory Garden

Black on White 93
Quicksilver Spring 97
Bourgeois with Bag 98
June, with Birds 101
The Inverted World 102
Victory Garden 104
My Wife's Back 106

I. NO DOUBT THE NAMELESS

CALL HIM ZERO

It struck them both as strange: although each pond and lake
clear to the coast was locked in ice, no open water,
the imperious wind kept pushing waterfowl *inland*. That night
a winter moon stood high and pierced the thin clouds' vapors
so the boy could contemplate their emptiness inside.
Relentless, the flocks flew westward. The border collie whimpered,
putting his forepaws now on one sill, now another,
as if some odd creature circled the house.
                                        This lifetime later,
a man, he looks back on that stay at her farm, its details clear,
their meanings still vague. His grandmother called it wrong as well
that the weather should be so frigid even in such a gale.
As a rule this kind of cold needed calm. He sees the fire,

the dazzle of sparks when she loaded a log. What seemed most amiss
was how the old woman's house no longer felt safe that visit.
He wanted and did not want to know what the dog might know.
He tried to picture the menace outdoors. He longed to shape it
so that he might name it. And after these many miles to now,
away from the ruby glow of the metal parlor stove,
from that blue-eyed collie, from the woman he so admires and loves
recalling that night; after so much time,
                                        he still believes
that to name a thing is to tame it, or at least to feel less bewildered.
Not *Death*, for instance, but *The deaths of Al and Virginia*, his parents.
Not the abstract legalism, *Divorce*, but *The disappearance
of my sweet wife Sarah, run off with that California lawyer.*

Not simply *Alone*, but *I have no children*. Was that the wail
of geese coming down the stovepipe? If so, it would be a marvel,
but he knew it wasn't. The caterwaul from the barn was alarming,
and more than it might have been had Grandma herself not startled—
after which she put on her late large husband's threaded farming
coveralls outside her housedress, which rode up and made
a lumpy sash. She stepped out under cloud and bird.
He would not follow. Rather, he stood
                                         indoors to wait
until she came stomping her boots through puddled barnyard holes
like a child herself, kicking ice shards to scuttle along
like beads from a broken bracelet. No matter. The world had gone wrong,
violent and void at once. She said, *The mare has foaled.*

On tiptoe, she read the mercury out the kitchen window,
then told her shivering grandson, *We'll call the new colt Zero.*

ANGLO-SAXON DIRGE

Few have been touched in this way   O strong broad hand that made
Those Sunday morning breakfasts   O Father shaper of biscuits
Whose palm on my shoulder soothed me   whenever life dealt me nasty

Hands like big Zach Storm   destroying my sandbox "farm"
Everything gone including   my pathetic "windmill" whose turning
Stopped when he snapped in two   the pinwheel whose parts he threw

Into the field-weeds' sprawl   Later I've been told
He snapped and stabbed his wife   That somehow fails to surprise
As I think of you father these days   it's as though I squint through a haze

That seems more and more to sprawl   over all I want to recall
Self-regarding the things I conjure   to others perhaps mere sugar
So be it   Your manner of gripping   each little finger lifting

The paddle in your canoe   like some satiric cartoon
Of a self-regarding snob   raising his idiot cup
Hands hauling guys of hemp   for that obsolete canvas tent

(Mother liked to call it your slum)   to raise it up   The fumes
Within of rodent urine   and human exhalation
Seem almost palpable   *To touch* is the etymological

Latin root of that word   *Stop it*   I think   *You're absurd*
Am I losing touch?   He's been gone   for forty years and some
All will go missing   forgotten   Is it only that I have so often

Said *I remember*   or do I   remember? Can I truly
Claim to catch sight in a biscuit   of your hand or swear that I miss it
In the bittersweet smell of wet canvas   that I see it along the surface

Of water calm and unruffled   or even within some cup of
Bitter campfire tea?   Such sight is abandoning me
Yes I do lose touch with time   I'd turn the whole sublime

sweet bitter saga over   to someone else no matter
I can't imagine to whom   I'd abandon the feelings too
To someone who might hold on   I want to but can't hold on

THE NIGHTMARES YOU KNEW

What would be worse, you wondered, a nightmare you actually pictured,
Or incubus, devoid of features,
Nameless, not even a creature?
No doubt the nameless. So you chose a few you could visualize.

If that's what you want, the nightmares whispered, and brought a digit-sized
Resplendent coral snake to slide,
All wriggle and toxin, inside
The house, your mind. The snake was the first to corrupt your slumber.

Then they decided upon a different guise altogether:
Scorpion, her claws tick-ticking under
Your bed. You heard. Small wonder
You felt so lonely, you felt so oddly accident-prone.

Gila monster lay, it seemed stock-still, alone
in the dim and dust-balled corner of the room,
like a heap of piebald stones.
The only sign that he lived: the cold stones' rhythmic pulsing.

She-ermine called you outdoors. You watched, you winced, recoiling—
In the deepest dead of winter, bone-chilling—
From red diacritics marking
The snow: pale page with umlaut and circumflex of plunder.

They made it into a shrike, or to use the argot, a butcher-
Bird, who deftly hung cadavers
Like minuscule, vivid flowers,
On any plant or shrub, whatever offered a thorn.

Then another something surfaced, which, with a languid turn
Of her erose tail, riled up the pond:
Swampland matriarch, fond
Of flesh, the alligator—all grin and fetor, ruthless.

Heavy-heeled, he trod the verges of northland forest:
Wolverine, possessive, dauntless.
He gnarred the wolf off the carcass,
Whose festering brain he consumed. On what was left, he pissed.

Be reminded: it was your will that made for all of this.
To envision each figure was to make it exist,
And you urged all to persist.
The nightmares are grateful to you for persisting too, no matter.

It's kind of you, they believe, to help them all to prosper.

NOT IN THE PHOTO (1952)

day lilies parched along flaking whitewashed walls
pale gourd hung on the porch   no wren inside
inside a hiss of cooking in smutted pans
we don't toss a baseball or wrestle my brothers and I
a far train's muffled blare

mother   father   an uncle   tiny grandma
arthritic old spaniel   wheezing in August weather
weather-browned fields   a shallow failing well
these things I gather could not have been posed together
fat Angus steers

stray again from the pasture to wander and blunder
the uncle does the same old trick with the coins
the coins disappear   who cares   we think   who cares
languid vultures aloft on the lookout for ruin
gray hazy air

EASY TO LOVE

Sean Malley owned a thrilling baritone
but in fact had range for any part of the four,
with a fifth thrown in by falsetto. We two were friends,
bachelors together. I did all right myself
when it came to singing, yet I wasn't going to be hired
for a Christmas solo, nor would the local Jews
pay me each weekend to rouse the synagogue
as they did Irish Sean the cantor. We envied each other,
but mine was the harder envy. What I'd have given
to open my mouth and become the very weather!
That's true, no matter I worried he'd die by forty.
It's stunning, the sort of thing you'll covet when young:

I'd have been Sean, huge as a barnyard boar.
I'd have been Sean, who was only short of revolting
because of the voice, which must somehow have needed
that enormous chamber of frame to resonate so.
He claimed he begrudged me only my girlfriend Susan—
my so-called girlfriend, that is—though often I told him
how she could wrap your heart into a tangle,
be with you now, now not, because in the end
you were only her whimsy. These many decades later,
I'm sure the fault lay less with her than me,
who craved some distinction beyond my hinge-hot bike.
Sean insisted he never envied that,

my bright silver Norton. Not that he liked his life.
He clearly didn't. But he didn't loathe it enough
to scrape it away on country road macadam.
Or so he swore. Who on earth would believe him?
Surely he dreamed of sweeping low through the curves,
someone like Sue on the pillion, her teeth so even
and feather-white even at night, her long hair streaming
red as a windsock sleeve, her arms wrapped tight
around your chest, her wine-sweet breath in your ear.
For my part, I'd have vowed a celibate year
to move the walls of chapel or temple like Sean.
(Celibacy would scarcely have made the year crueler.)

I think of a party when poor Sean snarled at me:
So here you are again with your movie star.
Lifting her helmet, Sue shook the famous hair,
cocking a hip at the gaping men by the grille.
She sweet-talked the hostess, who, lacking her own devices,
could only chatter back. Sean gulped his gin
until we coaxed him, as always, to keyboard and song.
Booze taking over, he lacked the normal control
that let him hold a note, it seemed, almost
as long as the party, with no quaver of sharp or flat.
Sean Malley was one of those singers who know by instinct
how the merest change of vowel will alter a pitch,

and how to prevent the slightest loss or gain.
That night, however, for reasons I think I see now,
he only growled some Tin Pan Alley corn,
then got up from his bench, announcing he'd be back soon,
waving our protests away. I wish I could say
I immediately turned to worry over Sean,
but in fact I was wooing that woman—or trying to woo her.
An hour passed, and he did come back, cold sober.
Tears stole through his tight-clenched eyelids as he chanted
something Hebrew and holy that none of his listeners knew
except Mel Feinstein, who couldn't sing and didn't.
It stopped our hearts like awful news or thunder.

Somehow just then I believed Sean would die, as he did
within months. Sick heart. Immensity undid him.
I held the bad feeling all through the tune he crooned
without any pause: old standard, "Easy to Love."
Everyone fell in love with love to hear it,
some weeping themselves until he quit again.
I couldn't have spoken for anyone else, but I knew
why this time I didn't hound him for further song.
A clear divide had somehow just been reached.
What was divided from what? I can't quite name it.
Sean hauled himself from his seat, the listeners parting
as if for a funeral cortege or slow-moving train.

In time the chatter re-started, all laughter and stories,
the guests drifting in and out of doors again,
some Motown funk replacing Sean's renditions,
our homely hostess replenishing plates of food.
Sean lingered inside and ate not a bite. Unlike him.
Susan meanwhile, as if to soothe my soul's
irrational envy, agreed to stay the night.
Meanwhile too, it seems, some villain had pushed
my beautiful monster Norton over the hill
to where I found it later, its wires torn out,
its headlamp crushed, hazed moonlight spilling through trees
onto its body, its saddle flung into the brush.

PALLID

—for my wife, from Lake Bled

Yesterday my Slovene friend,
dear Marjan, took me out in the country
to an amphitheater fashioned by nature
from palest marble. He wanted to show me
a second-century petroglyph,
Roman rendition of Mithras's bull.
The monument gleamed, a sensation no doubt.
But I looked on listless, as a lone drab dove
hopped stone to stone, each one as white

as this page I ponder. Now coasting swans
on the lake below show a different pallor
from paper or boulder or alpine snow.
I can't even render absence of color.
Blank? Bare? Ivory? Wan?
My words are black. It's all I can make them.
What value in them if we're not together
with these sights and bird-sounds and countless greens
of mountain spring? My banalities gather.

It's such a waste, I whisper, and flinch
as a swift kite skims, all wing and talon,
across the water, its shadow a menace
that flushes some ducks and an undersized heron.
My wasted witness. I'll soon be home,

but no account of mine will make
the things I saw and heard seem true,
or what on sensing them I felt—
no more than these forced lines will tell

how terribly I needed you.

A MAN TELLS A STORY

He described at the start how he bribed an older student
to buy the wine—rosé of course. Some sappy
song lay poised for the touch of the HiFi needle.
He'd lit four scented candles behind his curtains
to cast what he thought would be a romantic glow.
The flowers, he snickered, *were roses, needless to say.*
Oh, I was full of originality.

He almost believed the September breeze was panting
along with him as he crossed the quad to the bus.
Soon enough Sandy or Sally—the name doesn't matter—
got out, they embraced, then headed back to the dorm.
Meanwhile, disaster. The breeze had blown the curtains
against those candles. Steam leaked out of his window.
The firemen had already spooled their hoses and gone.

Not much of a blaze, he intoned, *but it was flame*
that doused our flame. He pretended to tear his hair,
then needlessly called his wrought up paradox
so much poetic bullshit—and there he ended.
These many Septembers later, I made for the porch,
looked across the fields to the star-pocked river,
and heaved a sigh as real as my laughter had been.

Like everyone there, I knew from the start they were done for.
But hadn't we all suffered broken hearts when young
and of course recovered? So this melancholy I felt
wasn't a matter of a couple's love gone wrong.

It was how in time we mock our very own dreams,
whatever they are. Our best laid plans—as the poet
famously called them—so often go down in flames

that we may think we've grown wise from watching them die,
that now we're seasoned enough for irony.
Such adult dispassion, however, is hard to distinguish
from resignation. Our little blazes spread
to places we never predicted, and when what's left
of all we longed for reduces itself to ash,
we shake our heads. We shake our heads and laugh.

COOKING BY WATERS: A NON-ELEGY

The birch's skin curls up like an ancient letter.
The sweet smoke makes my breathing harder.
On a streamside fir three goldfinches teeter.
Late sun makes a tumult along their feathers.
In an hour the hermit thrush will have begun.
I accept the bittersweet gift of the weather in fall.
The air's so clear the only haze is inward.
How did I learn these names and calls?
I can't be sure. They simply gathered.

Brook trout curled in the pan as the hot oil sputtered.
Back fifty years. Another sun.
Another scent. Another river.
The trout's spots slowly blurred.
If life is important then why is it light as a bird?
There's a version of loss I've long deferred.
It's a version that banishes elegy's turns.
I'm tired. I'm tired.
Let me climb like smoke into air.

I won't close my eyes looking down.
Down to where Donald Chambers fries the trout.
Done fishing herself a loon calls up the wind.
Without it there's nothing to lift her.
Darkness drops on the Middleground.
In smoke and absence my eyesight clouds.
Don is dead and gone.

So is Creston MacArthur.
Creston and I have dipped thirty smelt together.
Smelt from the Tomah River.

We rip driftwood from the brittle ice for tinder.
Our fire runs through its spectrum.
Steam rises beside it from our snowshoe leathers.
Seeking scraps a red squirrel fights a raven.
We laugh at that until we weep for no reason.
The water bears a sweet bouquet of tannin.
The chirr of the squirrel and the growl of the raven.
Rough as a bag of hammers says Creston.
We fashion such metaphors of construction.

Then they blow away.
Nothing's brought back or reproduced.
Or at least that's no longer my function.
By other later water I'm blinded at moments.
The lowering sun breaks through.
Are my tears caused by light after shade?
Or by knowing that words have such small use?
I will make myself stare at truth.
A heron takes its slow escalade.

Under faint early stars dark nighthawks dangle.
Bitterns boom somewhere.
Do these creatures ponder or care?
My cook-fire sends up its plume through the trees.
I hear the thrush's canticle.

It is raucous with ritual need.
Need a bit like mine.
Impalpable the smoke and mist.
What does the bird want to find?

Only her frail empty nest.

—*Washington County, Maine, 2012*

HOW TO SORT THEM

That woman's husband works the graveyard shift in a warehouse someplace.
He's a big man, and sleeps all day. I bet
he drinks. But what do I know? Dark clouds are stealing in.
Well, no they aren't. That's poetry, and bad at that.
She's a headstone color: gray hair, gray face.

Her hooded sweatshirt's dull, like a sheet of old tin.
It's as though she doesn't look forward to much but passing away.
Her eyes are gray too, though it's too easy
to call them empty. Their tears might so easily—flow. Oh no.
I'm fussing around for eloquence here and coming up empty.
The woman and I just nod at each other

as we wait by the post office window. Though I'm a rather old man now,
I go on looking toward some sort of future.
I'm a big man too, which may be why
that woman shrinks. Or I think she does.
We all like the postmistress, who's old herself but spry,

and despite her losses still cheerful and bright.
Her hairdo's new. I recall her husband, who was
a person people here always called Big Mike.
Some old folks claim the man could lift a barrel
brimful of hard cider right over his head. I'd like to imagine
some tribute to Mike. I'd write it, if that were feasible.

A character, Mike. He drove a truck
that he'd brush-painted pink. He lived with his wife and children
and a bunch of critters and mixed-breed hunting dogs far back

in the woods. In time the kids grew up
and moved from here, but the family, we remember,

seemed always so decent and gentle with one another.
The postmistress wears that shirt she loves.
It's a pretty shirt. Now what shall I name it? Purple?
Fuschia? Puce? And how might I sort them, good and evil?
How portray them? Let the clouds above,
the God-damned clouds, steal in. No, let them hurtle.

II. CREPUSCULE

OLD HUSBAND'S TALE

I ought to tell old husbands' tales, not wives'.
All my stories and I keep growing old
Together. Each of my friends and family has heard
For instance about my cold and dreamless night
In the deep Maine woods. I tell it year on year,

In a futile effort to summon a brilliant fear,
Which it seems I could only experience when young.
The charge of it is irretrievably gone.
I even tell the tale to myself, aware
Though I be that it will end in disappointment,

That the only remnants are physical: my ancient
November comes back with a squabble of owls, a chime
Of tuneful water through beaver dams, and time
So sluggishly crawling along that I, impatient,
Tear more limbs than I need from the thicket of cedars

To make a fire, by which I mope for hours.
Dark dropped so quickly that day it overtook me,
Then at dawn the eastern sky went pale to guide me.
In recollection, all my senses are there,
But no, the electric thrill won't come again.

A duller sort of fear has supervened
As other sorts of darkness and lostness loom.

My children are having children just in time:
There are days when they're all I could ever need, it seems.
Yet more and more in these latter days I am,

as the Bard so memorably wrote, the stuff of dreams.

LAST GRADUATE

She stepped forward and flipped her tassel across the brim
of the silly mortarboard,
and it seemed to him, *That's that*. It made no sense,
but he heard a closing door.
People later remarked that the day could scarcely be finer:

sky an exemplary, cloudless blue.
No one would call it hot.
No matter. Within his seersucker suit he was sopping.
He played at affirmation,
hugging her raucous friends, thanking her teachers.

Stop waiting around for magic,
he told himself, who hadn't really quite known
until now that's what he'd been doing:
waiting for something to put off the future forever,
its sorrows, which boded for all

and would make this grief look paltry. Still, she was the last
of the children left at home.
He faked a cough to cover another sound,
felt for his clenching throat
and pulled the necktie through an open collar,

as though it were time to relax.
He chatted with another parent, a doctor. It struck him

as odd that on occasion
he'd been this shockingly young man's patient.
A flock of geese overhead

gabbled, confused, broken out of its tight formation.

GATE, BEGGAR, AND BIRDS

*And a certain man lame from his mother's womb was
carried, whom they laid daily at the gate of
the temple which is called Beautiful....*
—Acts 3

As for me, I can only be carried there
by my own mind's eye,
which beholds the gate the apostle names,

all copper-sheathed
and high as these pines where I live. The gate
attracts the sun

as it dies on the column's western side.
Directly beneath,
the lame man sits, but I keep my eyes

on the fading shine.
I know little of what might be called divine,
but this afternoon,

from where I stood I likewise watched
the top of a mountain
while the very same sun that climbed the gate

reached the summit,
paused an instant, then dropped behind.
I watched and thought,

At least I know Beauty. But what does that make me—
a sort of tourist,
paladin of imagination?

The beggar will always
be sprawled there, both in fact and in vision,
in the sandal-stirred dust,

so I look off from impossible legs,
from unbeautiful hands,
cracked cups for alms. I want to linger

away from all that,
to savor the lovely, defined by what's fleeting.
Or so I say.

But today I heard a certain sound,
teemed with sad beauty,
a doleful keening: whippoorwills,

so rare these days
they're downright precious. I reminded myself
that in years long gone

that song was common
among these hills. It was everywhere.
And I scarcely noticed.

HETERODOX

A and B can't even remember
When they weren't friends   A knows B
Once had cancer   His hair came back
After the grim course of chemo   His doctors
Were persuaded they'd beaten B's disease

B's tall   A is sufficiently shorter
That not until lately has he noticed B's round
Of pattern baldness   though B's hair is back
Out of anyone's sight A kneels on the ground

The cancer's back too   *O God if you're there*
A whispers   *And truly can work wonders*
If the growth of B's hair can't again be normal
Let him come to shininess
As I have   A knows it's no common prayer

Is it wrong   he wonders   as ever conventional
To beg with his being's every fiber
That B may be thus strangely blessed
Natural baldness so suddenly crucial

KANSAS

We spend our years as a tale that is told.
—Ps. 90

Joey and I sit in The Prairie Junction.
He scans the menu then orders the "Prairieburg."
He's never been here before but it looks worth trying.

A man his friends call Marty just walked in.
Marty pulls up a chair next to Lorne and Rod.
They resemble a comradely flock of ancient birds.

I decide I'm going to order the chicken sandwich.
I haven't had it before but it looks good too.
I mostly want to know that there is God.

The men have on the clothes they wore to church.
Right after service their wives must have gone back home.
Bill jokes about the football team at KU.

Lorne and Marty laugh as though they mean it.
Shelly the waitress is a bit too loud but nice.
She's very young but she's laughing right along.

There aren't that many here but they all seem nice.
I call up a passage about the eye of God.
I want it truly to be on the sparrow, the eye.

I privately study the faces around their table.
Anybody would tell you that Lorne is handsome.
There's a certain rugged, hawk-like look to Rod.

Though he isn't handsome he appears to tell a good tale.
There's something in Marty's expression that strikes me as sad.
He looks to me as though something bad has happened.

Maybe it has but I have no way to tell.
His friends are being especially nice to Marty.
They may know the man has something painful to stand.

I know not a soul at The Prairie Junction but one.
We're not having much luck hunting out here but no matter.
It's good just to be with such a dear buddy as Joey.

We swap our own little narratives back and forth.
The men are of an age and so are we.
I don't want them merely cut down like the grass that withers.

They all have been inside their church this morning.
I bet that each has made it a habit to pray.
These men I'm watching believe there's God I believe.

And as for me I really want there to be.

WOODPILE TO SHED

—for Stephen Arkin

I swear that as a young man I could remember
every log I'd cut as I picked it from
the pile in our woodlot, loaded it, trucked it home
to the leaning tarpaper shed along with the others.

It was clear in my mind, I think, if the understory
had been thick enough that I needed to swamp it clear
so I wouldn't hang the tree I sawed mid-air,
and if wind had made the felling chancy or easy.

Like a subtle illness, this sorrow of fall where I stand.
I doubt I felt it all those years ago,
back in what I might call The Age of Cold.
Far more wood than I cut last spring was demanded

by a house unfit for winter, loose-shingled, drafty.
But the chore didn't daunt me. I *liked* to cut ten cord
with every April thaw. I could manage more
in those old days, and I admit to mute fury

whenever I stop to tally how much less
I can work up now. You'd think I'd learn to accept
a fact of life as sure as my own birthday,
or the deaths of my father and mother, or how in my forties

I gave up my paddling trips on true whitewater,
just for example, though I thought that signaled concern
less for myself than for all the children born
to this other, snugger house, tight-sided with cedar.

I check myself, on the point of shouting *Eureka*
as I pause to inspect the crooked stick in my grasp.
I do remember this one, hewn from a branch
of a tree I can picture as well, rough-barked but sleekened

by mist: a thin white ash on its dainty knoll—
or more precisely a gentle swell, a hummock,
what frail old Yankees here might still call a drumlin—
to which it had clutched by weak roots. No matter, I pulled

my saw into clamor. I might say *Tempus fugit*,
as someone bent on platitude might whimper,
comparing an early time in his life to a later.
That chunk of ash, pathetic in its crudeness,

will go on the fire tonight. The raw dark looms
behind a winter sky, the naked limbs
shudder and whine as breeze turns into wind.
The flames will help us to weather whatever comes.

CREPUSCULE

There's a man who owns two bearded collies.
On his drive back home from an office,
a widower passes the three at 5:30.

When winter afternoons go brief,
each dog is hard to see as it marches,
well behaved, on a leash.

As far as the widower knows,
they never cross the street:
it's always up one sidewalk alone

and then back down the same,
though maybe the man takes his pets
elsewhere at other times—

perhaps out of town to a field
to fetch a ball or stick.
The dogs may chase a squirrel

or find a brook and splash in,
their gray beards full of bubbles
that flicker, catching the sun.

The grass is so green in the widower's dreaming!
And those collies may flush bright birds....
The widower's driveway needs tending:

His daily commute has made ruts.
He'll see to all that later.
Meanwhile, what to heat up

For supper? Perhaps that leftover potato.

THE PASTOR

*I have just one person left on earth who's been
My friend through grade school, high school, church, and sports,*
The pastor says. Meanwhile the winter rain
Explodes on the metal roof like handgun shots,

And it's hard to hear the man go on: *Thing is,
He's lost his memory.* There comes a catch
In his throat, something that none of us has witnessed
Through all the pastor's ministry. He adds,

I'm left alone with the things we knew together.
Silence ensues, save for a few quiet coughs,
And rustlings of the worship programs' paper.
Then the preacher seems to change his theme right off,

Speaking of Mary, and how she must have suffered
When her son referred to his apostolic peers
As family, not to her or to His brothers,
Not to Joseph—as if He forgot the years

Spent in their household, as if He kept no thought
Of ties that bind. The congregants are old.
They try to listen, but their minds go wandering off
To things like the pounding rain outside, which is cold

And ugly and loud. The storm, so out of season,
So wintry, still improbably recalls
The milder months, which vanished in a moment,
And which they summon vaguely, if at all.

MILTON'S SATAN

Diabolical heat for that time of year.
A fan whirred and hissed.
A digital clock blinked on its table.
Self-will was pulsing:
I ached to fly off and find the last of our children,
gone too far away to college.
The nest was empty. Burned. The ceiling

of her room still showed its poster for *Some Like It Hot*,
shriveling after long years
when Monroe looked down on a herd of plush deer
and other mild creatures
now ragged with age. I imagined imagination
might cool my soul: I wrestled to mind
a gentle meadow dotted with flowers,

the checkered shade of a hardwood stand in fall,
a small brook's ice-jeweled pools,
and last, an unmarred quilt of snow
on our cellar bulkhead.
Such willful visions wouldn't hold. The meadow was scorched,
it was tunneled by rodents, and parasites thrived
in the tree-trunks, mosquitoes would hatch from the streambed.

The snow looked pure but mercury laced its flakes.
Her absence was bodily ache.
It throbbed. It scalded. There were reasons to think of Satan,

his imperious will,
will's ruinous conflagrations. *Which way I fly,*
Milton's devil claimed, *is hell.*
Satan said, *Myself am hell.*

WINTER POET

Again the full moon climbs, precisely on time.
What else would it do? A shame that as it floats
it doesn't spark interior commotion.
Or perhaps it does in its way, but what it produces
is no less familiar by now than moonlight on snow.
Fireplace wood, well aged, neither cracks nor hisses
but makes a soft dull hum. He's just come to
from a doze, with another man's book of poems on his chest—
which he sets aside. He suspects if he opens it now
he'll shut it. Not that he won't find time to persist
in reading it later, having little else to do.

He watches as shadows extend themselves on the lawn,
chimeras too. He's tired of tired old tropes
using shadow and light. But what does he want at his age?
He's seen enough to hold to what he's got,
to the lovely, faithful, intelligent woman he owes
for what at its worst is contentment, and even his cat,
who after a nap of his own seems focused upon
an angle of parlor baseboard. If he longs for his children
to be children once more, for instance, he knows they're gone
to live with their children, and all his magical thinking
will never transform them to rosy infants again.

Perhaps this is more than anything else what unnerves him:
that memory's his topic, that he can't resist it
and seek out something more lively. This afternoon,
inventing a chore to cure his idle brooding,
he revised his ragged address book, which largely consisted

of rubbing out names of the dead. He'll be a witness
to more burial ceremonies now than he will to weddings.
Not that *memento mori* should be his motif,
since that's as hackneyed a theme as a fat moon's rising.
He hates his incapacity to behave
or express himself these days without ironizing.

He'd like to dream as he used to some absent lover
and how he'd been wronged by her, by the world's meanness,
the witless incomprehension from those around him
—dull, bourgeois like him now—of his colorful pain.
As if that kind of thing had ever seemed less
a commonplace either than the stale return of moonlight.
He still can muster the laughably easy sort
of phrasing he once thought fresh: *There you will sit,
lonely, adjusting a lamp, as I step abroad
into moonshine.* He almost sees the lover fret
over things that he could explain to her were frauds.

THEY'LL LEAVE FIRST

A fire warms the tipsy room where we're all gathered.
It's the first time any of us has invited *them*—
as we've come to call the two—since that awful *then*
when the tumors took their only child, a daughter.

The talk's been mostly idle, our little group
guarding its words, every one of us keeping
relentlessly away from anyone's passing.
What good would it do to bring their nightmare up?

We want to believe that our prudence implies our sorrow,
but we mostly loved the child because she was *theirs*.
In time, we'll summon only details: her hair,
bright as a fire-truck, her gleaming, glossy grin

encased in dentist's steel. They assumed a future,
those trips to the orthodontist's. They were worth the cost.
We'd all have done the same. You'd expect their loss
would by now have blighted or at least have marked their features,

but in fact the two seem almost devoid of expression,
his face opaque as he straightens a leaning candle,
hers as she centers a vase on the granite mantel.
It's late, and the world of professions and obligations—

like getting children to school and back home after—
dawns on the younger guests. We ritually praise
the splendid meal, and reassure ourselves
that it's so much fun to get together, our patter

boding a general exit. They'll leave first.
The host and hostess joke that, come tomorrow,
they'll tie their daughter up to her piano.
A recital's coming, and by God she'd better rehearse.

As we look for our coats, we notice a pile of cards
scattered, precisely, on the high-gloss lid that guards
felt-gloved hammers, nickel-encased steel strings.
Has somebody dealt a hand, and if so, when?

We'd surely have noticed some interloper here,
having been together from cocktails through to cigars.
There seems no accounting. But *they* assemble the cards,
turning them all face-up, then tapping them square.

FINAL EVENING AT OXBROOK CAMP

Our loons still scull on the pewter
calm of the lake, the chick having dodged
the eagle one more day.
The valorous drake and hen both held it
between their bodies while the raptor circled.
Reprieve. And here I am, old.

I stooped an hour ago
to dump the pail of dace I'd trapped,
then watched them scatter, the ones
we hadn't hooked through their dorsals for bait.
Twenty or so now swim at large—
still prey, but not to us,

Who are headed home in the morning.
I'm poised to throw away this clutch
of wilting black-eyed Susans
picked wild by my wife of all these years
to grace our painted metal table,
where we lifted ladders of spine

from fat white perch, last supper.
So here I am, this aging man
who wants somehow to write
only one love song after another.
I pause at dusk, I blink, I toss
Our dim bouquet into late summer's woods.

III. WHEN THE LIGHT FAILS

PARIAH

It's March, and my usual Sunday walk for the paper,
bread and milk, whatever,
was more like a creep. The storm had laid a scrim
on the ground and turned it into an icy desert
that some mystic hand appeared to have littered with trees,

which groaned in agony.
Would the ground-feeders make it? Had the burrowers been locked in?
Jack Green and his brothers conspired to beat
Joe Green, some distant kin,
almost to death not far from here last week.

I fought for balance, feet feeling for purchase.
The Green boys mauled poor Joe because they thought
he'd turned them in for poaching.
They ought to go to jail. There really ought
not to be such outlaws among us.

It was well past the season for deer. The Greens had done nothing
to ascertain they'd found the right culprit.
If we normal citizens were plotting
vengeance, wouldn't we check our facts?
The Greens were drunk and likely figured, *Fuck it.*

So two brothers grabbed Joe's arms and pinned them back
while big Jack shattered the architecture
of his cheeks and one eye socket.
Just imagine if Liz the pretty teller
from the bank hadn't passed and phoned the cops,

or if some other business elsewhere had held them up.
When I ran into Jack in the store,
he knew I felt what I felt. He was sober and clear.
He knew I was one of a lot
who felt the same. He dropped his eyes to the floor

and buried both raw hands
in his dung-rank pockets, quick as he could, a motion
that somehow brought to mind
the frantic efforts I've noticed in frightened rodents
as they dive back into their dens.

Those were hands that roughed up little Joe Green,
and those were hands
that Jack and his brothers use to claw a living
out of their roughed-up land.
The trial is set for April. Soft as snow,

Jack whispered to me: *Hello.*
I've read that desert clans will starve their sinners
by chopping off right hands,
the ones used to scoop out food at the tribal cook-fire
where the great pot stands.

I didn't answer Jack. We all just want some peace.
The road back home was sheerest ice.

OLD CREATURES

I don't care that my good old neighbor can hardly hear.
His is the voice I crave, not mine. Just now he talks
Of something he hasn't before, and it's more than just a shock
To get his grandfather's story. The man worked forty years

In a sawmill, even after he cut his leg off below the knee.
A bunch of them carted him home, and he let the stub bleed dry.
Lord, I think, what might that mean? Why didn't he die?
But I keep my mouth shut. He didn't die. *He took a tree*

And made a leg. I mean he took and hollowed out
Two foot of the trunk, and then put in a mess of springs
To cushion the meat, with a shoulder-strap to hold himself in.
My neighbor laughs. *By Jesus, there was a tough old goat!*

You heard him coming near half a mile away. I could scream,
Because once with a chain saw I cut myself in the thigh.
But I got carted to the spanking hospital where I
Took a hundred stitches and staples and sucked morphine.

They don't make them like they used to. The cliché rushes to mind.
But where we live today anyhow, they really don't have to.
The plummeting sun backlights my friend through his parlor window.
He's only a shadow now and a voice, his words a kind

Of under-current to the thoughts I'm thinking, which as usual tend
Where they will. I suddenly picture one of our dogs who's blind.
He's waiting for me at home and staring all wide-eyed,
As if to concentrate would make him see again.

At length, we'll have to put him down. Despite his champion
Bloodlines, he's a runt. Still, what he's always lacked in bigness
He's made up with brains. It's sad to see that uncanny brilliance
At a loss, although he seems less given to depression

Than puzzlement at his condition. I used to swear
Over having to listen so often as that midget whoofed and whined,
Or rather almost spoke, so close were his various sounds
To actual words I could sometimes believe that's what they were.

Now I pity him, hearing in his voice what may be anger,
Less at lack of sight than at the insufficient
Clues to the loss he feels. Where's an explanation?
Of course he can't fashion his eyes' replacement, as the grandfather

Of my ancient neighbor did his leg long back.
                                                 I rise
To say a word before departure, but then, despite
The galloping dark, I see with my own still viable eyes
That my old friend's sleeping, as if he had willed the speechless night.

LOCALS

i. Arrogant

All of us knew the old fool. Or didn't know him—
it's just that each winter we saw him out on our pond,
thin as a straw, with his stiff white moustache and his sissy
rimless glasses, which he'd stop to clean on a shirttail
after he'd steamed them up by repeating his trick,

his one dumb trick. Hands locked behind him, he'd glide
a while—and we admitted the old guy could skate—
then he'd go spread-eagle, his feet in a sort of wide *V*,
and rough-cut a circle. He'd go on to cut some others,
spin after slow goofy spin. He had the sense

at least not to wander out to our end of the quarry,
where we beat on a scarred old puck and on each other,
boys somewhere between fifteen and seventeen.
That New Year's Eve, after dark, which of course came early,
we made a fire on our shore out of sticks and crates.

Somebody'd brought the beer and puke-your-guts-out
strawberry wine, so we all were well along
when the pageant started. Who put the show together?
None of us gave a damn. We looked across
as some tiny figures began to flicker and stagger—

like images shown on a damaged movie reel—
past the neater fire that burned on the opposite bank:
kids, it was easy to tell, because they'd have fallen

if their fat-bottom fathers hadn't kept holding them up
from behind, hunched over, clutching their little elbows.

Then several pairs of untalented, elderly dancers
came wobbling out. Some 40's music crackled
from a record player the adults had rigged somehow.
We hockey players snickered to watch the finale:
that skinny old man, in what looked like a Zorro suit,

complete with cape. Holding some sort of baton,
he went to the fire, where he spun in his usual way,
and in the process lit that stick in his hand.
He moved to a smudge pot, spun to light it too,
then on to eight more pots that someone had put there.

Who'd have done *that?* It didn't matter. We sneered
at *oohs* and *aahs* that reached us there where we gathered,
stamping our feet and knuckle-punching each other.
We got the idea: The Merry Village Lamplighter
or some such idiot mush.

                                                    He must be dead

many years by now, and most of us have children
older than we were then. So when I imagine,
as I sometimes do, the old man's pivots and spins,
and the cluster of pots he left in their glowing circle,
a wonder and beauty flare that didn't back then.

ii. Positive

Things just changed back then. *Shit happens,*
as the saying goes. It was over that summer.
We'd split the custody of our children.

That puny circus came back to town,
I took the kids, and there in the stands
sat poor old Leon with a group from the home.

I thought my life was hell in those days,
but Leon's example should have cured that moping.
He had to deal with a lot more than I,

and no end in sight. When I waved, he smiled,
I think. One side of his face wouldn't bend.
By now he'd had his condition a while.

The three of us watched some hay-belly ponies,
unshod and shaggy, shamble around
the single ring. Their one and only

trick: to stand on two legs. They did it
a dozen times, then trotted out.
Leon's companions appeared to love it

and stood up too, the ones who could,
and cheered. I saw Leon move his lips
and I knew from before just what he said:

Yes, his only word since it happened.
A man came to clean up after the ponies,
same bastard who'd loudly counted my children

—just two, after all, a boy and a girl—
when I showed my tickets. He'd come again later
for some ham-fisted juggling of clubs and balls.

Happy? I asked my daughter and son.
Puzzled, they nodded. I pictured Leon
outside his barn, a pail in each hand,

nodding his understated hello
when I'd drive by his farm. Even well, he was modest.
I tried to forget him again all through

the acts that followed: the contortionist,
the clowns and acrobat and strongman.
For the children's sake, I played optimist,

saying *Yes* to everything, just like Leon.

iii. Ignorant

It must have been hard for Nick
to stay positive in that shop,
his father-in-law's garage.

Nick was my longtime friend,
his side of the story my side.
He always seemed to confide

in me for some unknown reason.
He'd shake my hand each time I stopped in,
which old Yankees rarely do.

So you'd think I'd have heard of the ulcers,
But no, I didn't know.
No one learned what it was

That killed him until it killed him,
Nick wouldn't see a doctor.
Stoic, country-stubborn.

The death made me think of how
I'd once caught him clutching his gut,
leaving a torque wrench to rattle

and dance on a fender a moment,
as if that were some sort of trick.
Nothing but heartburn, he claimed,

turning aside my questions,
turning to what really hurt him:
how his wife and three young sons

obviously favored her father,
while Nick was the one who worked
out straight every night and day

to keep the family going,
including that very same father,
who lounged indoors on a couch,

a man so goddamned stupid,
—as Nick would often complain—
he don't even know how to ache

whenever he's in pain.

iv. Philosophic

He ached for absolutes
but life remained a woeful riddle,
So he left it behind. No note.
Just an empty vial, snarled sheets and quilt.
He had no family anyone can think of.
As if it consciously tricked him,
the world showed him only encrypted symbols,
which at last he grew tired of decoding,
or tired of not knowing how.
My thoughts about him are, of course,
themselves a sort of decoding,
though I knew him well. Or I thought so.

Who knows anyone, really?
No doubt it's trite to wish there had been
something I might have said.
Should I have offered my witness, say,
to joy in the flow of the normal,
in seasons coming and going, in birds

that crowd the skies in migration?
I look outdoors just now,
earth unveiling itself
for spring. Above the river, a throng
of snow geese. I also hear the chirring
of nervous, agile red squirrels.

These phenomena mean nothing
beyond my desire to assign them meaning,
if that describes what I do
with such facts. The plain fact is,
I miss the man, for all his endless
contemplation of life's conundra—

endless and useless. I shudder too,
appalled by my own imagination,
in which I see him waking again
to this little town he lately abandoned,
gone quiet after heavy snow,
even the letters on postal boxes

written in script he doesn't know.

v. Drunk

We didn't know Ross had been out to the lake—
He flipped his truck in the snow coming back—
But you read almost all of his life in the wreck:

In the upside-down cab, smelt flipping in booze
From the two broken fifths in the torn brown sack,
Torn Powerball tickets floating there too,

And moldy Kentucky Fried Chicken bones.
He landed head down among those scraps,
Not hurt. His license was already gone,

So a new violation, though no one was counting.
I'm still his friend, whatever that shows
About either man. *I don't have no fucking*

Problem, Ross says, *except everybody*
Sticks me under a microscope.
He's got no problem. *The cops all judge me—*

So do the judges. They know the names
Of his wife and his ex, and both women know
What'll be what when Ross wades home.

If you can believe it, one time from jail
He made his free call to 911.
He told dispatch he was being held

Against his will by desperate men,
And *the whole damned gang of them packing guns.*
Why can't everyone leave him alone?

I wish my friend's wild escapades
Were all as goofy as that prank with the phone—
Not stomping some other barfly's face.

He had it coming! So Ross would shout.
I cussed at Ross, I called him a fraud,
I told him again he'd better dry out.

Ross just repeated, *I got no problem.*
I long for a way to get him on board,
So I prod him about his wife and their children.

His second marriage is sinking fast.
I doubt it, but that's a thing that might
make him see his life for what it is:

a sea of whiskey. He keeps doing time.
Short time so far. I dream him dry.
It has to be hell to live like him.

He's in a fishbowl, and people are spies.
That's what he thinks, though we all see him come
From 20,000 leagues away.

vi. Natural

I said *yes* to myself as I passed that way,
yes to the cans and shards by that trailer,
to a dead toaster's guts, which had simply been flung
through the doorless doorway,
yet which seemed somehow *arranged*
among the clods and clinkers and rocks.
My life has been distilled to details,
but on balance has been exquisite,
no matter I'm the one to say so.

I pictured the unlikely whiteness
last spring of a weeping crab
beside that so-called mobile home,
framed by its bashed-in picture window,
beyond which, inside the shell,
to be sure, lay deep, discomfiting darkness.
Leaning now against a wild apple,
sleep in my bones,
I consider all this, ignoring blood

on one of my thumbs from my carelessly grasping
a thorn-bush to help me up
the steepness to here, where it's getting on dark.
I can't stay all night,
though apart from arousing concern
in family and certain others who'd care,
where would be the harm?

This October's not cold, I don't feel pain,
my blood-beads are strangely pretty.

In a clearing halfway up,
I came on a predator kill: ruffed grouse,
subtly luminous plumage
making a trick of the light, almost
a pattern. Nothing—no beauty, no good
in a life—comes entirely for free.
A barred owl starts its eight-note chant,
far enough off to sound plaintive, not clownish.
Others might hear all this and say it:

A life like mine is hardly exquisite.
                        Maybe *I'm* the clown:
these redundant climbs, my hikes and rambles
with no ends beside themselves,
which will end one day.
Each to his own,
but if those mockers had come with me
they might in time think back on
that ivory shower of the crab tree last May,

or even the junk, or the grouse's feathers,
or how twilight tonight
glides smoothly along toward absence of light,
soft odor of evening falling,
this tempting drowsiness too,
all the grander themes died down.

They might remark on the curious privilege
of hearing a solitary apple
make a gentle thump

here on the good wide welcoming ground.

WHEN THE LIGHT FAILS

So little was left of my aged friend that autumn. His shadow showed
all chiseled in the dooryard against the lake when the moon was more than half.
In the chop the water's surface broke like a mammoth tract of ice
into sharp-edged slivers. The light's supposed to save us. I'd tip the shade

to see his backlit outline. His daughter'd been dead for ages. Who'd think
that a heart could fail in a girl of sixteen, that so much pain would follow?
His son Big Mickey came home from Viet Nam, he said, as crazy as God
knew how to make him. Now this. No reason anymore to thank

that God or hate Him, he claimed. He'd sit all night out there in the wind,
which usually calms come dark but didn't that fall. The next son, Bo,
was long dead too, for all his valor, fighting the muscular dystrophy,
working each day till he fell, but rising. Then at last not rising. My window

framed him, near motionless as the pines behind him, which paraded
in their standstill file along the seawall he'd built, a pick and prize-bar
his only tools but hands. Whenever he stirred, it was slow as he ever
moved in his blinds for the ducks of October. It looked as if he parodied

the gestures of some other person. He felt in the pocket of his woolen pants
for his bottle and pulled it out, his arm inching up, his head back-tilting
—then he did all that in reverse. I was so damned helpless. I wasn't magic.
No one blamed his wife for raising hell when she came on those pints,

always empty, or almost empty, although he tried his best
to stash them out of anyone's sight. This latest death, he swore,
was the load that broke the critter's spirit, no matter it didn't break hers,
a woman who knew the identical grief. *That booze is sure a beast,*

he admitted, *but seems the ladies do better when life bears down.* I know
it does bear down. No, I don't really know, thank God. And now that crazy
Little Mick had shot himself. My friend said his grandson's gun
went off unexpected. A whole town did expect it, but my neighbor said no,

bad accident. Meth, we knew, wasn't that. In the mornings, he'd sweat,
he'd shake like a wormy puppy. It ate up my heart, still does. He was always
so full of life. He's gone, and I—I keep coming back to the light,
prettily winking in water behind him, having pared him to silhouette.

SHE RECALLS A BOOK OF SAYINGS

For some reason she's moved by his chilly withdrawal
To search for a fitting proverb.
Why this one? *Stay from among wild fowl
If you fear the wagging of feathers.*

He jostled the china from her old wedding shower
As he made his bumptious way
To the crepitant hearth. She whispers *Fire
Won't be hidden in flax.* Her bouquet

When she flung it was caught by an old-maid aunt,
Who twitted: *After a wedding,
Beware a corpse.* A joke, a taunt,
But she still feels her own foreboding.

Their wedding trip lulled her at first to imagine
Proverbial wedded bliss.
She had never known birds or sand so dazzling,
Nor yet known this restiveness.

As they strayed on that luminous beach arm in arm,
The passersby must have witnessed
What looked like young love. But come full dark—
The palms in their sudden stillness

Like milliner's plumes—unnerving sensations
Fluttered into her heart.
She could never quite find the right words to name them,
Nor quite complain that they hurt.

At trip's end—it shocked her—their talk turned to anger,
Which at home soon became automatic.
They were scarcely civil to one another,
Though they rarely grew histrionic.

After this late quarrel, hunched, vulturine,
He strains to exude self-control.
Through a living room window, she sighs as she sees
Their small twin girls, who roll

And flail in new snow, making side-by-side angels,
Then, watching a raven drop
From a leafless blue beech at a murderous angle,
She gives the window a rap.

She longs somehow to set the world back
To what had once seemed right.
Now pale dawn, for instance, portends something black,
And the calmest of skies unquiet.

Truth shows best naked, she thinks. A mirror
Grows dark on the chiffonier,
In its glass a vague image, which rapidly alters.
First feathered. Then shrouded. Then bare.

OUTSIDER

A gigantic Kubota tractor drags
a rotary mower
at highway speed down the timothy field
along our river.
We're driving toward unhurried, expensive Sunday
breakfast out with friends and family.

I brake for just a moment to sight
down the stubble swath
the tractor has left as it carves another.
I could stay and watch
for week upon week, and yet I'm sure I wouldn't
know just what to feel. I envision

a group of sinewy men—all blood
relations, I'd say—
with long-hafted scythes. They'll work until noon
to lay down the hay
that the big machine has just sheared in a matter of seconds.
Then I picture a later farmer who reckons

how many more hours will disappear
before he can finish
his task with the horse-drawn sickle bar.
The day will vanish
into black and he will have cropped just half his field.
How did those workers feel?

Did "feeling" matter? I blink and sigh
and go on my way,
too old by now, I hope, to imagine
Good Old Days,
that witless myth, with its claim that exhausting labor
in those times made men and women better.

That strikes me as the very sort
of sweetened belief
contrived by people who haven't ever
toiled in their lives—
farmed, or done much with back and hands at all.
And what about me? I do recall

bone-wrenching summer jobs I took
when I was a boy
on an uncle's place: I planted fence posts,
I heaved baled hay,
and so on. Now I cut five cord of wood
to dry each spring inside our shed.

But it's not that I have to work that way, nor did I
in those summers either.
I don't know much, though I did know this place
when it was a diner.
Today quaint tools are hung on its walls as examples
of *An older time when life was simple.*

That's what it says on a placard. A two-man
crosscut saw.
A harrow disk. Ice-tongs. An auger.
At least they know
how they feel, the sentimentalists. I order
Cider Crepes with Hand Churned Butter!

SOLITARY

—Christmas Season, 1958

Bev pulls the shades on outside things—the weeds
in empty pastures, poking through last night's snow
to make a shadowy pattern like a wind rose,
sun that bores through the low matte clouds,
as if a sleep-shut eyelid failed to occlude
unwanted light. If she ever prayed, she'd pray

away the thunderous plow of the highway crew,
the men's probing shovels. Let no one come this way
with face aglow, bearing some useless present.
Let every one of the townsfolk stay at home
and wonder, *Why on earth is she so alone?*
Their ignorance of her life makes for contentment.

She's cheered by the winter climate's storied dangers.
She wishes them worse. She knows if people breach
her solitude, they'll unglove hands to reach
inside her soul, it would seem. Let snowdrifts gather
and seal her deep inside her willful fastness.
Come in, she thinks, *and welcome, storm and darkness.*

HOME

—in mem. Glen B.

It's a funny sort of a business,
he began. I'd let him run on.
I wouldn't interrupt him.
I intended my quiet as a kindness.
Outside I heard heavy traffic,
heavy for here anyhow.
He always done what they told him.
He slouched in that ratty recliner
he'd owned all the years I'd known him.

I tried not to notice the stump,
which of course didn't reach to the footrest.
He made sure he carried an orange
wherever he went, right on him,
in case he got faint. Even loafing
to home he done that, he said,
when he got through working for Cal.
And he stayed away from the sugar.
Not only some sugar—all.

He'd rigged himself a contraption
to help him: two-by-four frame
with a rope-loop that hung from the crossbar.
He could sit up by grabbing the noose.
Outside the traffic seemed louder.
He joked that the cat on his lap
were the last of his livestock now,
and she weren't no bother. The bother
were to pee day and night in a bowl

and to prick a finger each morning
like they told him. Cal's farm had that corn-piece,
he said, but they used it all up
for them box stores, not far from his home.
He weren't going to let himself mind,
he weren't going to mumble and moan,
but the lights from the lot and the cars—
daytime or dark didn't matter,

you didn't see stars no more,

you barely could find a full moon.
Of course there were some things better,
he admitted, his stub be damned.
He had to keep to home now,
but there sure were a lot less pain.
Different ones didn't like
those stores, and if you asked,
he weren't that fond himself,
but things just come to pass.

He huffed as he chinned himself up.
You can't stop progress, they claimed.
Argue on that if you like,
he'd live with the change, whatever.
If you can't stop something you take it,
like he couldn't stop diabetes,
goddamn it all, and excuse
the goddamn parlay-voo.

He done what they said. No use.
He spoke of how he'd follow
his hound up Tuesday Mountain
in old times like it were a stroll.
It's damn near a miracle now
just to make it across a room.
What with the leg, that was—
or without. He chuckled, I resisted.
I didn't feel quite at home.
Outside a semi downshifted.

Bernice flew off of the roost
before he even turned fifty,
and their kids grew up and skedaddled,
one clear to California.
Bernice—she had her reasons,
and he knew it. He weren't no saint.
He knew that too, but he'd stay
to home now. *Home,* he whispered,
whatever that meant these days.

FOREVER

She wonders if it's cliché to think of the husband
with whom she's lived for decades,
most of which she'd call, all things considered,
a pleasure—if it's cliché to imagine her partner
as a ship at the lip of a clouded horizon.

In fact he's sailed the whole way over.
And then she wonders why she should wonder this.
What difference whether her metaphor's trite or fresh?
And what does she know about ships?
Early on, as they sat one morning together,

he felt in his pocket for car keys,
held them up against the kitchen's skylight,
whispering "Cockney. Cockney."
It passed, they embraced, both a little uneasy,
but he went off to work as always.

For what seems far too long they kept it away,
didn't mention that morning, conspired in its absence.
After all, there seemed nothing
that either could do about it then, and nothing
of course to be done today.

What does she know about ships, about sailors?
No, nothing either,
though once as a girl she was carried out on a bay
in a rich friend's yacht. The cold white spray
flew across the beam. And there's more that she can conjure:

they all could have slept in the boat's big cabin
in comfort, if that had been part of the outing's plan.
The tiller was made of such dark lovely wood,
and everything else on board
seemed some bright metal fitting or shiny brass lantern,

and the life-rings that hung on the rails
were stenciled *Claire C*, the name of the boat.
It all made her feel she could never want anything more
in the way of beauty. That gleam. That air.
He had had beauty as well

back when he was the young man she chose
to live and sleep with ever after.
They made children together. They said they were blessed.
The beauty, which changed with the decades, was nonetheless
beauty. She still supposes it so,

though it swamps her soul
to watch him sink out of reach, unheeding.
Why can't she call him *up?* Why can't she call him *to* her?
Her mind shifts back to her girlfriend's father,
who kept talking about a crack in the sleek sloop's hull,

no matter his pretty wife's counsel
that he relax, that he live for this day
of wheeling seabirds, foam and speed,
sharp-edged, slam-bang clouds,
clamorous squeaks and snaps from mast and mainsail.

But how he worried, her husband!
He insisted it might be only a matter of time
before that tiny fissure turned into much more.
He was looking for something to do about it there
and then—as of course he couldn't.

He said he hated to think of his treasure,
Claire C, beyond saving, to imagine the day
when off it might be
—he used the cliché—
to Davy Jones's locker with her. Forever.

BLUES FOR THE TENOR MAN

—Washington, D.C., 2013

You guard that treasure with a fierceness as great as your playing
Is masterful. So I imagine. I see it's a Selmer,
Top of the top of the line, the kind of sax
You could pawn for at least a grand—no, more than that:
Even ten wouldn't cut it. I see your pants belonged
To somebody else at one time, their shredded cuffs risen
To display a strange blue latticework of lesions
On ashen shins. The paper placard's scrawl
Is HELP IM A HOMELESS VET. I'd never have thought

You smoked, and a pipe of all things. Its wet rough stem
Pokes out of your Navy pea coat's rough side pocket.
You're so good you make some better part of me float
To a long-closed club, with someone like Sonny Stitt
Sweetly trotting his horn through "The Sunny Side
Of the Street," which happens to be the song your Selmer
—Above this tuneless traffic—sweetly offers,
Quietly but so intensely I'd bet the flesh
Under your woolen hat must actually flinch.

Raveling watchcap, it creeps on your head, it shivers.
I might of course recall the other Sonny,
Or the great Coltrane, or the under-prized Lucky Thompson.
Jack and I played them all in that student apartment
Where, kids that we were, we imagined ways to resolve
The world's most unaccommodating problems,
Of which, at least to us, Racial Relations,
As people said back then, were among the first.
We were children, but worshipped the art that Roland Kirk

Had dubbed Black Classical Music. And here you are
To push me back to reverie and reverence.
You slide straight into a blues in a minor key,
Blues new to me. Eyes clenched, you rock and sway,
The tenor igniting the stars. Blue pigeons drop
From government marble, as if their tiny brains
Understood the mix of resolution and pain
The music spreads around their strut. Their plumage
Seems to glow more warmly now, yet the damage

That anyone's life can attract appears more clearly,
Brightness cutting the dark: that's the way of the blues.
But what do I know? I'm headed off for a meal.
To hand you a coin would somehow be to feel
A lesser person. I wonder where Jack lives now.
The Lucky, the Coltrane, the Sonny, and hundreds more:
They were gems we'd gathered from hockshop and secondhand store—
And were stolen one night. If only we'd kept up our guard.
It wouldn't have happened if only we'd known how to hold

Onto what we treasured. How suddenly things can be taken,
Though a record collection is only a record collection.
You'll huddle beneath whatever wrappings you gather
Against the cold of night, the noble Selmer,
The pearl of great price, locked on your chest with both hands
As you sleep. Or so I imagine. As evening steals in,
Your horn moans an aching cadenza that ends the tune.
Commuters pour downward into the Metro, unhearing.
The pigeons flap roostward. Soon there will be nothing

For you to lie down with again but what you love,
Under a bridge, in a shelter, wherever you live.

AUTUMN

Why not write something for those
who scratched out improbable livings here?
Someone has managed to sow
This broken field with stones, it appears,

So someone's scratching it still,
Although that Japanese knotweed has edged
The tilth. Two wasps in the chill
Attempt to catch sun on a rail of the bridge.

The old local doctor has passed
At almost a full decade past ninety.
He never seemed depressed.
Seventy now, if barely,

I consider the field again:
Someone will drag these rocks away
But they'll be back. The air smells like rain,
Which is fine, the summer's been much too dry.

Nothing is left of the barn
But some rusty steel straps in some nasty red osier.
The stone fence still looks sound,
But even there the knotweed steps over.

Hadn't I pledged an elegy
To the old ones who worked here? You couldn't claim
They thrived, exactly, but maybe
They likewise scented good wind full of rain,

Lifted eyes above this old orchard
To the cloud-darkened hills and found their support
Somehow, somewhere. No matter,
They kept going until they could go no more.

The trees' puckered apples have gathered
A flock of birds, and as they alight,
They're full of unseasonable chatter,
As if to say that all will be right.

The old ones I promised a poem
Must have said it too. *It'll be all right.*
I never knew them. They're gone.
I say it out loud, *It'll be all right.*

—*Caledonia County, Vermont*

WHO KNOWS? THAT LIFELONG QUESTION

i. He Risks a Walk

Between two pock-marked beech, on a strand of wire
For cows he recalls from childhood, the cruel barbs shine,
Small blooms of brightness. When darkness stoops, Orion
Will glow as he's always glowed among the stars.
He'll nock his arrow, as if he meant to stir mayhem
Below. For now, the old man thinks of the house,
Where his wife must still feel disquiet. The weather scared them
Last night with a sideways rain that in due course froze.
When he comes upon a winter-kill, he wonders,
Has he read at some point of a people who buried their dead
As this poor ruffed grouse is buried, neck and head
Alone protruding, or was that just some old torture?
The grouse's stiffened crest is lustrous with frost.

The bird had hidden in powder. When it turned to ice,
It sealed the body in. So peculiar a sight
Has stopped the old man cold in his foolish walk.
Today's no day for wandering under trees
Exploding around him everywhere loud as guns—
The clap and crack of bursting limbs and trunks.
Sunbeams garland the forest in silvery beads,
Every branch and bole, both shattered and whole,
A radiant filament. He can't see why
Death should be brilliant. Its dead eyes rimed and white,
The head might be a flower, or maybe a jewel
Carelessly dropped by somebody roaming where
The old walker feels his way, the trail so sheer.

ii. He Walks and Stops

The trail so sheer, his knees not what they were,
The walker finds himself
Pausing more often than stepping, and in these lulls—
Although he's tired of memory,
Which is mostly habit, and has been the stuff of his life—
The past creeps up again.

He muses how it's the biggest surprise he's known:
The fact that he's gotten old,
That, for example, he's forced to put a hand
On each of those cobbly knees
And push down hard whenever he needs to step over
The most modest swell or rock-form.

It's what he did on grammar-school stairs, he recalls,
And then, in adolescence,
Went on to mock the younger boys for doing.
He sees those little ones still,
In untucked shirts and jeans and untied shoes
Gone muddy from the playground,

As they pant on the steps, their little mouths agape,
The dread, imperious bell
Reminding them they're late again, they're late.
The old man also sees
In this grove of oak a few stumps here and there
Of long-gone trees he hewed

Maybe forty years back. Their wood has all turned dozey,
Such that he almost pictures
Their turning to air itself were he to kick them,
Although of course he won't,
For fear of losing balance. Imagination,
Picture—it's all he has,

It seems, by which he means the ceaseless function
Of memory, selective.
He thinks of war in Syria now, for instance.
He ought to concern himself
With that, or any news his mother referred to
Once as "current events,"
Rebuking his idle dreaming. He hears her voice
To this day, can't contradict it.
Three cord in eight short hours: that's what he'd fell
And cut and split and stack.
Why shouldn't he still be strong? Surprise, surprise.
He walks on fifty feet

And pauses once again. A random gust
Blows in a scent of winter
He can't identify, though it's familiar:
He's taken the odor in
For seven decades, but now he wants to ignore it.
He'd rather not be mired,

Even for one short moment in the least old question.
Yet how does one look ahead
Or out from here? The very prospect strikes him
Absurdly. Still he notes
The buds of February tending to purple
The way they've always done,

And he can't help it: he has to envision spring,
Somehow he can't resist.
Is this mere habit too, or might it be
Some actual sense of revival?
He walks a while again and stops again
And walks and doesn't know.

iii. He'll Stay With That

He doesn't know as he walks,
that two coyotes mate
within yards of where he passes,
in that late-growth fir clump northward.

He just knows enough to imagine
they're there. If he passes again
in eight weeks or so, the bitch—
if she exists—will howl.

She'll be guarding her whelps from the walker
unless or until he moves on.
If she feels fear, she'll hide it.
Out on the river, ice

will have loosened up its suction
to either shore, and he
may not witness this either. Who knows?
Who knows? That lifelong question.

He tries not to prophesy
what constitutes his future,
but silently urges himself
to consider what little he *can* know,

or at least can see: for instance,
those tiny, wriggling specks
in the granular stuff under trees.
They're snow fleas, harbingers

of the sugar maker's season.
Perhaps he'll stay with that,
will end with sweet figuration
as home rises into sight.

IV. VICTORY GARDEN

BLACK ON WHITE

Whispering *Snow at last,*
I pause and smile
from the low, north-running ridge
along our pond.
Winter so far has been
a grim collage
of gray on gray, last autumn's
leaves all glued
to one another, clutching

the dismal ground.
Even in sunlight, the woods
and fields stayed somber,
outside matching or making
my inside life.
A friend across the river
has lost his only
son to homicide,
and no one knows

a motive, except perhaps
joy in the tire iron's death-blow.
Most of my neighbors mutter of what
the world has come to,
though it's come, I think, to what
it always was.
Still, talc-white flakes are sifting
gently through
the canopy of pine,

the sun-disc—curtained
by snow—looks like some outsized
pewter paten,
and beatitude spills down
on me despite me.
The gun-gray ice of the pond
has disappeared
beneath the cape of white,
which remains unmarked,

inanimate, until
a minuscule vole
turns up to slither along
the top of a drift,
apparently legless, as if
a serpent but benign,
if matters of good or evil
were relevant here.

The rodent's utter blackness
seems blacker for where
it shows, and I can imagine
nothing on earth
so dark. And then there's something
darker: a raven
crashes onto its path
to block the rodent.
The tiny vole stops dead,

its maze of tunnels
behind it, back onshore.
It has nowhere to go.
More like fearsome raptor
than scavenger,
the great bird slams its crude
wedged beak again,
again, again, again,
the way some berserker

might his blunted weapon,
the victim whipping
its body back and forth.
Then it lies
on blankness, still as a clod.
The murder achieved,
the murderer flies away
to a blighted maple
to bob and squall, indifferent

to its kill. I clamber
down and inspect the corpse,
stretched beside
its own blood's scarlet scrimshaw.
Yet I can't insist
that even this dark event
has darkened my mood
or caused a change of heart.
The world is only

what the world has always been,
and in this tableau
I see—do I dare say it?—
a beauty some painter
in her deftness might have captured.
The force we call nature:
I can both hate and love it,
after all, myself
being both in and of it.

QUICKSILVER SPRING

how can the red-winged blackbirds come back
so quickly to croak from wetland cattails
and the ditches run so soon with snow
from hillsides amid that odd leather odor
beside the freshets and all of these take me

to late April mornings some forty years gone
when I'd drop the only child we had
back then at school who ran out and whirled
on the merry-go-round in that muddy yard
working up his fragrant sweat

while rasping he-ravens overhead
whirled and fought among themselves
for she-ravens perched in the leafing woods
as skunks began to roam again
like the one I saw on this much later morning

poor sad creature clipped by a car
dazed mid-road with blood in its mouth
and something I swear that could have been tears
in its eyes which swept back and forth as though searching
for what could have happened so quickly and how

BOURGEOIS WITH BAG

I ease my laptop down its leather throat.
How many times have we boarded planes by now?
The bag's been with me so long I never figured
On buying it how perfectly it would fit
A computer. I'd never even used a computer,
Just noisily tapped away at my Smith-Corona,

Machine once dear to my heart. Where is it now?
I churned out poems that summer, a rich foundation
Paying our Tuscan rent. I've kept the bag
Through sharper changes than techno-revolution:
The children grown and gone, the grandchildren born,
The myriad wonders. It makes no sense at all

That the bag's soft runneled hide, the straps more slender
Than a woman's bra's, the buckles bent by age—
It makes no sense that they comfort me whenever
I feel them. Still, they do. The bag was hanging
In the alcove window of a Sienese sporting shop
Deep back in an alley, safe from a humbling sun.

I wasn't looking at all for something to soothe me.
Through the gloom of shade, I saw its leather shine,
Like an icon of any youthful man's desire.
It's ridden with me for nearly thirty years.
The proprietor said it was meant for ammunition,
Though what hunter would use it for bullets I can't imagine.

It's seen a hundred classrooms, five hundred lecterns.
Last night I pulled a few new poems from the bag—
Some late attempts at whatever I'm trying to say—
And read them aloud to a gracious Texan crowd,
Which included a writer my age I much admire,
Who during the Q and A announced out loud

My work reminded him how deeply in love
We all should be with earthly things that die.
But the bag never judges whether I'm what you'd call
A success or not, just sits beside me, patient,
In buses, planes and cars, quiet bearer of all
Those efforts at meaning. This thing must know me, I think,

However absurdly. *Inanimate*, I whisper,
Yet something in me supposes it otherwise.
Nothing has been so full of my private existence.
It's scarcely spectacular, that hidden life,
But I feared for it, and the public one as well,
When I walked outside to the street, my reading ended.

Some twenty rounds of small-arms fire broke up
The air around the corner from where I stood.
I held the bag to my chest like a shield. I'm better
At a bourgeois sort of existence than any other.
The past, says the old cliché, swims by one's eyes,
And so it did, the finer part: the marriage,

The children, the children's children. I all but cried—
And now I can smirk at what some call poets' "courage."
This is the only life I've ever owned.
Through much of it I've held to my ammunition
Pack, a keepsake from when I dared to presume
The world was all before me—as in fact it was

In another way from when I thought the years
Would be stuffed with nothing but fervor. As in fact they've been,
Just differently, as I say. So here we are,
Leaving the Dallas airport, still mostly sound,
My bag and I. Not long till we take to air.
We're on our way now. Soon we'll clear the ground.

JUNE, WITH BIRDS

—for Fleda Brown

I know a vernal pool that last night's storm refilled with water.
Ferns already stood there. This morning I came on ten square yards
of tannin-tinged basin quilled with fronds, with a yellow fringe of warblers.
That seemed adequate magic. A cat's-paw sighed, then chased off after the birds.

I found strawberries in a burn, their leaves bright freckles on cindered earth.
The fruit got crushed in my shirt, but when I took the pocket to my mouth
and sucked, the world went spinning more blithely. And even though the first
discovery of my hike, minutes after I set out,

was two dead robin chicks in their nest, those berries were still all sweetness.
For years I've traced, and hope to retrace, that climb. From a hemlock up there
—its bark all gone, its trunk turned to punk, its branches stripped of needles—
fell sudden salvos of laughter: I saw the same old woodpecker pair

(those berries tasted of sadness too, it feels almost needless to say),
come back again with bursting June to the same familiar tree.

THE INVERTED WORLD

So there I was in my truck, just ducking a wire
—harmless, a telephone wire—that last night's storm
had slung low over our driveway. I caught my wheels
downside of a bank I couldn't even see
because of the brush, which by now had gone withered, brown.
There wasn't a thing I could do. It felt so *slow*,
that rolling over. I watched a small bird flit
across the road ahead, backlit by sun.

One mammoth oak must once have been struck by lightning,
to judge by the flare of scar just under the crown,
bright orange ringed with black by shock and heat.
I'd never noticed before, but then again
I'd never looked up through a windshield quite that way.
Of course I had plenty of time as well to curse
myself for being stupid. And yet I didn't.
I heard another voice—no, I can't say

a voice, but something (don't ask me what or why)
insisted right along on something else.
My garage friend Cory came with wrecker and cable,
put my tires back under me, and set things right.
Soon I detected some lack, some hunger, it seemed.
What was it? This much later, it's hard to tell,
and if I try, no doubt I'll get it wrong,
the whole affair still strange as the strangest dream.

Did I fleetingly disremember what age must bring?
Did I really lose sight of friends who'd either died
or were on their way to dying? Could I have watched
that bird or that evening sun, which floated in
to soften the woods? I think I pictured my wedding,
so blessed but decades old, as if it were now.
The world in those instants appeared somehow to get better
by way of vision, memory, and forgetting,

and of being, however briefly, upside down.

VICTORY GARDEN

Here I go again as ever moping on Things
That Vanish alas this time for no reason whatever
those wheels of cheese under clear glass domes
displayed on the counters of general stores all vanishing too
it doesn't take much to start me I'm driving back
from our own town's uncheesed store with the paper

and its freight of awful news from everywhere on earth
and I wonder just how long that earth can survive
but I'm moping too that my wife came home
today with a desk that once belonged to her vanished grandma
and looks to be as heavy as fifteen anvils
and it's 90 sopping degrees outside

the globe burning up and I'll be sweating lugging that load
my hands both useless against the deerflies' blitz
which will get me down too and we don't have room
anyhow for this monster   I'm 70   I need to be getting
rid of things not taking them on and this morning
I picked what seemed a hundred ticks

from our dogs   we never had ticks here not until lately but now
I pass Polly our lovely old neighbor a bonnet her shield
against those ticks and flies unmindful
of any such nuisance as she weeds her garden and she looks up
all proud of her work you can tell and kneeling waves
and offers me a friendly smile

as if someone had told her *Say cheese* and as if in spite of headlines
like the one I saw at the store when I glanced at the paper
Husband Runs Over Wife With Tractor
while her funny and ornery husband Tink in spite of lumbago
stands some yards behind her in their shed to sand
a mammoth sideboard so lost in his labor

he doesn't see me not that he needs to

MY WIFE'S BACK

All naked but for a strap, it traps my gaze
As we paddle: the dear familiar nubs
Of spine-bone punctuating that sun-warmed swath,

The slender muscles that trouble the same sweet surface.
We've watched and smiled as green herons flushed
And hopped ahead at every bend, and we've looked up

At a redtail tracing open script on a sky
So clear and deep we might believe
It's autumn, no matter it's August still. Another fall

Will be on us before we know it. Of course we adore
That commotion of color, but it seems to come
Again as soon as it's gone away. They all do now.

We're neither young anymore, to put matters plainly.
My love for you over thirty years
Extends in all directions, but now to your back as we drift

And paddle down the tranquil Connecticut River.
We've seen a mink scratch fleas on a mudflat.
We've seen an osprey start to dive but seeing us,

Think better of it. Two phoebes wagged on an ash limb.
Your torso is long. I can't see your legs
But they're longer, I know. Phoebe, osprey, heron, hawk:

Marvels under Black Mountain, but I am fixed
On your back, indifferent to other wonders:
Bright minnows that flared in the shallows,

The gleam off that poor mink's coat,
Even the fleas in its fur, the various birds
—The lust of creatures just to survive.

But I watch your back. Never have I wished more not to die.

ACKNOWLEDGMENTS

The author extends thanks to the editors of the following periodicals for their support:

Agni, Artful Dodge, Ascent, Café Review, The Christian Century, Dark Horse (UK), The Georgia Review, Great River Review, The Hudson Review, The Journal, New Ohio Review, Numéro Cinq, Pinch, Pleiades, Plume, Poetryzoo, Shenandoah, The Southern Review, Spiritus, Tar River, and *Theodate.*

Sydney Lea is author of eleven other volumes of poetry. A former Pulitzer finalist, a recipient of fellowships from the Rockefeller, Fulbright and Guggenheim Foundations, he was founder and longtime editor of *New England Review*. He has also published a novel, a collection of literary criticism, and four volumes of personal essays, most recently *What's the Story? Reflections on a Life Grown Long*. His work across the genres appears in some fifty anthologies. Active in literacy and conservation efforts, he lives in northern Vermont with his wife Robin Barone.

Publication of this book was made possible by grants and donations. We are also grateful to those individuals who participated in our 2015 Build a Book Program. They are:

Jan Bender-Zanoni, Betsy Bonner, Deirdre Brill, Carla & Stephen Carlson, Liza Charlesworth, Catherine Degraw & Michael Connor, Greg Egan, Martha Webster & Robert Fuentes, Anthony Guetti, Hermann Hesse, Deming Holleran, Joy Jones, Katie Childs & Josh Kalscheur, Michelle King, David Lee, Howard Levy, Jillian Lewis, Juliana Lewis, Owen Lewis, Alice St. Claire Long & David Long, Catherine McArthur, Nathan McClain, Carolyn Murdoch, Tracey Orick, Kathleen Ossip, Eileen Pollack, Barbara Preminger, Vinode Ramgopal, Roni Schotter, Soraya Shalforoosh, Marjorie & Lew Tesser, David Tze, Abby Wender, and Leah Nanako Winkler